**Ins**

Poems by David Glover

Illustrations by Cheryl Lucas

Insect Poems

ISBN: 978-1-910181-10-2

Published March 2015

First printed March 2015

Printed and Published by Anchorprint Group Limited
www.anchorprint.co.uk

Contents

241

Ant

If you listen carefully
You'll hear me puff and pant,
I race around your garden,
I'm a busy little ant.

I'm ready in the morning,
By the time I leave the nest,
My feet have little trainers,
And I wear my running vest.

I run between two paving slabs,
But there ahead a trap,
I dodge the paws and the mighty claws,
Of a very hungry cat.

A giant pair of leather shoes,
Approaches on the trot,
It's then I run for cover,
Underneath a flower pot.

Soon I'm hiding in the grass,
Away from blackbird raids
A mower tries to mince me,
With it's ever turning blades.

Now the mower's gone away,
I'm safe here once again,
But I should have worn my Wellingtons,
It's just begun to rain.

Each raindrop is the size of me,
And soon the lawn is brimming,
Of course I could have drowned there,
But instead I took up swimming.

I swam back to the patio,
Then ran back to the nest,
At last I put my feet up,
For a long awaited rest.

Bee

I'm sending out a signal,
So people know it's me,
Buzzing everywhere I go,
A happy honey Bee.

Suddenly I'm quiet,
As I'm now in ecstasy,
Enveloped in the blossom,
Of my favourite apple tree.

My legs have gathered pollen,
From those stamens everywhere,
My little wings will struggle,
To transport them through the air.

At home the place is buzzing,
Bees are busy so alive,
It's there we're making honey,
In our very own beehive.

Precision engineering,
Is employed inside our home,
Creating little chambers,
For a perfect honeycomb

We have to keep on schedule,
For it's now we know the date,
The village is preparing,
For the annual summer fete.

They turn up on the Saturday,
On foot and in their cars,
And there they buy our honey,
Which is now in little jars.

by David Glover and Cheryl Lucas

Caterpillar

I'm hairy short and wriggly,
You'll find me on a leaf,
Sometimes I'll be there on the top,
Or hiding underneath.

My jaws are always aching,
So often do they bite,
Eating leaves the whole day long,
An endless appetite.

I have to hide from time to time,
Or be sandwich filler,
The birds might feed me to their chicks,
Who dine on caterpillar.

When I'm finished eating,
I become a chrysalis,
A suspended little package,
Now whoever thought of this?

The glory then of springtime,
The sun up in the sky,
And then as if by magic,
I become a butterfly.

They refer to me as admiral,
Promoted I would say,
They're full of admiration,
When my wings are on display.

Fly

I flew in through the window,
For a challenge I must try,
A challenge somewhat risky
But I'm fearless I'm a fly.

I landed on a home made cake,
Now tell me I'm a clot,
The baker nearly got me,
With a very early swat.

I flew around in circles,
Then I landed on his neck,
The hand that came to get me,
Nearly dropped me to the deck.

I rested on a pelmet,
Then I landed on his nose,
Next a swipe with all his might,
In fact he had three goes.

I tickled hairs along his arm,
Another game of mine,
A rolled up paper smacked his arm,
I flew off just in time.

Then I raised his hackles
When I landed on his cheek,
And what the baker said to me,
I simply can't repeat

I must speak to my neighbour,
For he told me such a lie,
He said 'I know the baker'
And 'He wouldn't harm a fly'!

Flea

This time I'm even smaller,
As tiny as can be,
That's why my name is not too long,
I'm simply known as flea.

I'm living in your curly hair,
Right there upon your head,
And later when you're sleeping,
I'm curled up inside your bed.

It's nice and warm beside your skin,
And nothing else will match,
But still I must be careful,
Just in case you need to scratch.

And if I need some transport,
Then I'll ride your dog or cat,
To find my friends now living,
In your carpet and your mat.

I live in fear of vacuums,
Especially now the steamer,
The only way to save myself,
I jump on to the cleaner.

So if one day you feel an itch,
Before you scratch beware,
Spare a thought for little me,
Now in your underwear!!

Lady Bird

I gaze into the mirror,
Where such loveliness is seen,
My beautiful eyelashes,
I can flutter I can preen.

Then I use mascara,
With eye liner round my eyes,
Which are of course quite stunning,
Like the stars up in the skies.

Next I must be careful,
With my full protruding lips,
Painting them precisely,
With the finest of lipsticks.

I wear the latest fashion,
Tailored velvet and it's red,
On which I place the black spots,
From a box beneath my bed.

Then I meet my best friend,
And as strange as it may be,
Like the vision in my mirror,
She's identical to me.

Snail

I simply won't be hurried,
For my pace of life is slow,
Today I must have travelled,
For a meter don't you know?

This morning it was raining,
Yes the weather it was hell,
But I was warm and cosy,
Here inside my homely shell.

I'm something of a gourmet,
In the things I like to eat,
A course of leaves will always please,
And grasses are a treat.

A pal went out to cross the path,
And then I heard a crunch,
The blackbird came despite the rain,
And took him out for lunch!

This afternoon the blackbird,
Came and tried to frighten me,
He pulled and pulled but I held on,
He won't have me for tea

I love it here in England,
I was born here just by chance,
But I've heard of others boiled alive,
And eaten there in France

One day I hid inside my shell,
Beneath the garden bench,
Someone was sitting right above,
And clearly speaking French!!

Slug

You wouldn't want to touch me,
For I am the ugly bug,
I'm long with flab and slimy,
And I'm simply known as slug.

You might of course be clearing leaves,
Which gather on your land,
To discover that you've picked me up,
I'm lying in your hand.

Soon you're in the kitchen,
With a lettuce you have grown,
And there you find me on a leaf,
I'm actually in your home.

You wouldn't want to eat me,
So you throw me back outside,
Again I'm in your garden,
Where my family all reside.

First we have the baby slugs,
No bigger than your nail,
Cared for by the adults,
Who can leave a sticky trail.

Then those in retirement,
Counting wrinkles on their skin,
Caused by basking in the sun
When they were young and slim.

by David Glover and Cheryl Lucas

Worm

My place is subterranean,
I struggle through the soil,
I must have drawn the shortest straw,
To put up with this toil.

To make it worse a proper curse,
The roots down here keep growing,
I need a torch and a pair of eyes,
To show me where I'm going.

Before me then a barrier,
A pile of old brick rubble,
I need to go to a hardware shop,
And buy myself a shovel.

Whenever it is raining,
I hear claw steps up above,
A blackbird tries to find me,
Saying 'Come up here my love'

Below I pass a wedding ring,
And later felt my loins,
Rub along the edges,
Of a stash of Roman coins.

Then an empty bottle,
That once was full of beer,
A pair of smiling dentures,
I discovered very near.

On to another garden,
The reviews all said it's fine,
The soil was lush with rotting stuff,
And lots of dung this time!

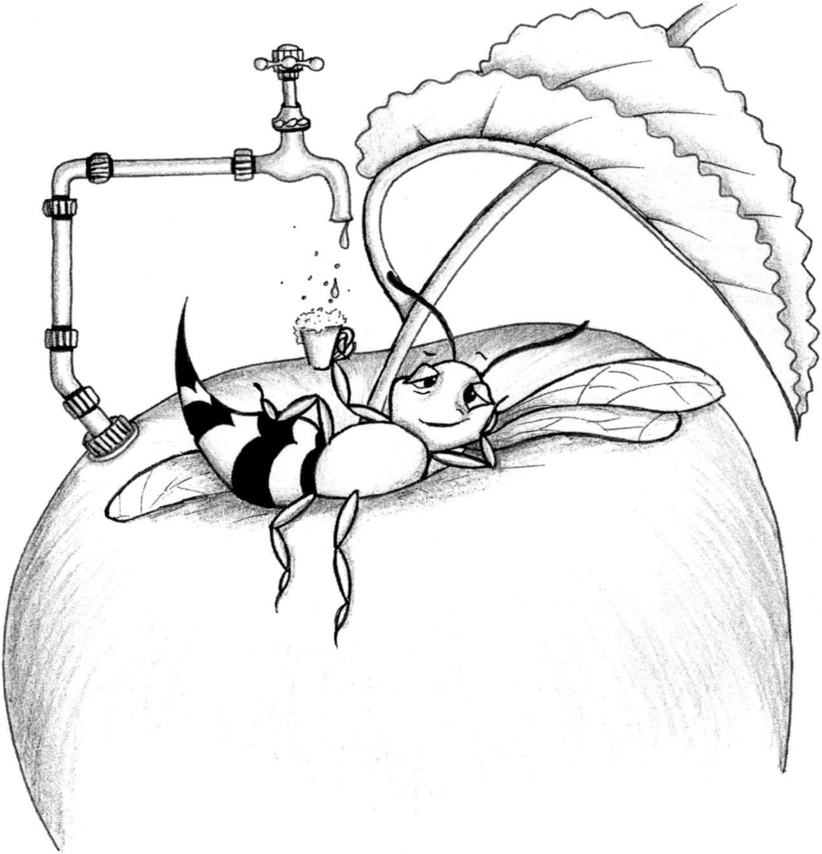

Wasp

I clear a room in minutes,
Striking everyone with fear,
Causing them to panic,
Just to know that I am near.

They recognise a certain buzz,
When I am on the wing,
And raise their expectation,
That it might be them I sting.

They come back for a battle,
With their swats and nasty sprays,
It's my turn to be careful,
Or they'll end my salad days.

I remembered all those lessons,
Which I learned at flying school,
Diving climbing banking,
And escaping as a rule.

The only thing to stop me,
Is the taste of something sweet,
All the jams and honey,
Are the things I like to eat.

Once I'm in a jam jar,
I can eat at such a rate,
My stomach starts expanding,
'Till I'm clearly overweight.

Then I need a tipple,
From the cider apple tree,
My head is feeling dizzy,
After drinking two or three.

Along the branch I find a place,
It's hollow like a trough,
My legs give way I close my eyes,
And there I sleep it off.